OUR PERFECT FATHER

Understanding God's Ways

JAMIE RODRIGUEZ

Copyright © 2021 by Jamie Rodriguez
All rights reserved.

First paperback edition July 2021

Originally written July 24, 2018

Book design by Jamie Rodriguez
Edited by Lee Roberts
Interior Design by Michael J. Williams
Cover photo by Jessica Wong on Unsplash

Unless otherwise indicated, all Scripture quotations taken from the (NASB®) New American Standard Bible®, Copyright © 1960, 1971, 1977, 1995 by The Lockman Foundation. Used by permission. All rights reserved. www.lockman.org

Scripture quotations from The Authorized (King James) Version. Rights in the Authorized Version in the United Kingdom are vested in the Crown. Reproduced by permission of the Crown's patentee, Cambridge University Press

Scripture taken from the New King James Version®. Copyright © 1982 by Thomas Nelson. Used by permission. All rights reserved.

ISBN 978-1-7372610-0-1 (paperback)
ISBN 978-1-7372610-1-8 (e-book)

www.burningfirepublishing.com

DEDICATION

To my Father, Jesus Christ, with love.
-Jamie

TABLE OF CONTENTS

Introduction	7
1. *Fear & Respect*	9
2. *Spoiled Christians*	13
3. *I Told You*	19
4. *An Empathetic Father*	27
5. *The Teacher*	31
6. *A Father We Can Trust*	37
7. *A Grieved Father*	41
8. *The Perfect Father*	45
9. *A Saving Father*	51
10. *Our Father's Love*	63
11. *Our Humble Father*	69
References	75

INTRODUCTION

At an early age, around my preteen years, the Lord started tugging at my heart. I was struggling to overcome the person I was and the person I didn't want to be. It was also during these years that my family, like all families, started going through some really tough times. Those times would end up being some of the best times—I will forever be thankful for them. God used those times to start building the foundation for our relationship. We truly became Father and daughter. I turned to Him and, in return, He was there for me. He gave me a deeper understanding of the things that were taking place in and around me. This understanding helped increase my love, faith and hope in Him. I had my family and church family to help me through, but the pain and hurt were too deep and the battle was too strong. I had to turn to my Heavenly Father for help.

When I was 12, my mom asked me to read Psalms 27 every night before bed. I believe this was all God's doing because this Psalm is where my spiritual journey with Him really began. One verse always stuck out to me, *"When my father and mother forsake me, then the Lord will take me up."* (Psalms 27:10, KJV). As a young person, I began to understand that no matter what I go through and whether or not my parents are there to help me, God will take me up! He will be there to deliver me from anything; I can always count on Him. From then on, through His Word and through experiences, He has shown me all the ways He truly is my Heavenly Father. My heart's desire is that everyone would experience the amazing and loving, parental qualities of our Lord Jesus Christ. I want to share what He has shown me and taught me so that more people can learn to love Him, respect Him, and trust Him in their lives. I pray that this book will be a blessing to all who read it and that it will draw you closer to our Heavenly Father, Jesus Christ.

FEAR & RESPECT

What does any parent want from their child? They want love and respect, for them as well as for others, which is why we were taught manners. Sadly, love and respect are diminishing with every new generation. Love is growing colder and colder and, as a result, respect is getting more and more rare. Genuine respect requires some level of love.

Some adults had it rough growing up. They learned respect, but they didn't learn love. There was not a proper balance of teaching respect and obedience out of love. A child can respect or obey out of fear of punishment, yet not so much out of love. That is not our Heavenly Father's way of parenting. If we obey Him out of fear, then what happens when we are no longer afraid? Let's think back to when we were growing up. What happened when we weren't afraid of our parent's consequences anymore? We rebelled and said, "I don't care, I'm gonna do what I want to do! They can do whatever they want to me!" Eventually, fear runs out and rebellion sets in. I'm not saying that we rebelled because we did not love our parents. What I am saying is that when controlled by fear, we don't allow the connection of respect and obedience from a place of love. Our Heavenly Father wants us to obey Him out of love, not fear.

Growing up, I told myself I didn't want to do something because I didn't want to disappoint my parents. Needless to say, I still disappointed them many times, but the difference is that it hurt and I felt sorry for it. We should feel the same way about our Lord Jesus Christ. We should not want to disappoint Him. When we do, we should feel bad about letting Him down because we love Him. This is the kind of relationship our Heavenly Father wanted with His children from the beginning.

> *"There is no fear in love; but perfect love casts out fear, because fear involves punishment, and the one who fears is not perfected in love."* (1 John 4:18)

> *"Fathers, do not provoke your children to anger, but bring them up in the discipline and instruction of the Lord."* (Ephesians 6:4)

In the Scriptures, our Heavenly Father asks us to fear Him. But this call to fear is not to be afraid of Him; it is a call to respect Him. Simply stated, to fear God is to respect that He is God and we are not—that He will stand by His Word. God is saying to respect that He knows better than we do and that when we cross the line, we will have consequences.

If we are taught to honor and obey our earthly parents, then how much more should we honor and obey our Heavenly Father?

"Children, obey your parents in the Lord, for this is right. Honor your father and mother (which is the first commandment with a promise), So that it may be well with you, and that you may live long on the earth." (Ephesians 6:1-3)

Honor your father and mother because it comes with a promise of a long life on this earth? Doesn't that promise shadow the promise we have from our Heavenly Father if we honor Him? We receive everlasting life after this world passes away. The same way we are commanded to honor our parents is the same way we are commanded to honor God.

"A son honors his father, and a servant his master. Then if I am a father, where is My honor?" (Malachi 1:6)

The consequences we had as children were meant to teach us a lesson so that we would learn not make the same mistakes again—to teach us to choose what is right. We may have been afraid at the thought of our parents being ready to punish us for our wrongdoing, but we were not afraid of our parents in general. Our Heavenly Father is the Creator of consequences, yet the purpose has never changed.

Parents are human beings; they are not perfect. Thankfully, the same cannot be said for our Lord Jesus Christ. He is the perfect Father who gives us the perfect balance of love and correction. We learn to respect and obey Him out of love, which results in us loving and respecting others.

> *"Hear, O Israel! The LORD is our God, the Lord is one! You shall love the LORD your God with all your heart and with all your soul and with all your might."* (Deuteronomy 6:4-5)

> *"'Teacher, which is the great commandment in the Law?'*
> *And He said to him, 'You shall love the Lord your God with all your heart, and with all your soul, and with all your mind.' This is the great and foremost commandment. The second is like it, 'You shall love your neighbor as yourself.' On these two commandments depend the whole Law and the Prophets."* (Matthew 22:36-40)

To love, fear, and obey God is for our own good. After all, He knows best.

> *"Now, Israel, what does the LORD your God require from you, but to fear the LORD your God, to walk in all His ways and love Him, and to serve the Lord your God with all your heart and with all your soul, and to keep the LORD'S commandments and His statutes which I am commanding you today for your good?"* (Deuteronomy 10:12-13)

2

SPOILED CHRISTIANS

We've all complained about what we don't have or what we want or need at some point in our lives. Some have even thrown spiritual tantrums and gotten angry when God didn't answer their prayers right away. "Why God, why won't you just give me what I'm asking for?!" We don't understand why it's taking so long and become frustrated. We find ourselves being impatient and upset with God.

We were told no so many times growing up, sometimes with an explanation and sometimes without. Either way, we had to be satisfied with the answer or lack thereof. Remember how frustrating it was not to be able to do something and not know why? Especially, at a young age when we want answers to all of our curious questions. Blind obedience seemed so cruel at the time, like our parents were just being plain mean not to give us an explanation or maybe we didn't agree with the explanation. Some of us may have even told our parents that they were mean. Why *couldn't* we go over to our friend's house or have that toy we really wanted? Was it so wrong? Maybe not, but maybe our parents knew something we didn't or maybe they could forsee the result was not going to be good for us in the end. In truth, they might have been actually trying to spare us from harm or even potential danger. At the time, we didn't have the knowledge and wisdom of our parents in order to know what was best for us. In the same way, we don't have all the knowledge our Heavenly Father has in order to understand what is best for us. We don't always see eye to eye with Him either because, after all, we think we know what is best. Don't get me wrong, He lets us in on His knowledge through His Word; however, when we don't receive what we're asking for and it's not clear exactly why, we have to trust our Father instead of throwing a tantrum.

He has good expectations for every one of us as He tells us in Jeremiah 29:11, "*'For I know the plans that I have for you,' declares the LORD, 'plans for welfare and not for calamity to give you a future and a hope.'*" Don't all parents have expectations for their kids? Why is it that God's expectations seem so dreadful to some people? As it goes in life, not every child meets or wants to meet the expectations of a parent. In our case, however; living according to the expectations He lays out in His Word means eternal life for ourselves. We can't meet His expectations of holiness on our own. We need His Holy Spirit to help us.

Sometimes people live like God is obligated to conform to their lives instead of the other way around. When would a parent, who allows their kid to ignore the rules and do whatever, whenever they want, result into a respectable, responsible adult? We should not be spoiled Christians; we should be sanctified Christians. Our focus should be on our purification and conforming to God's ways rather than the blessings He can give. Our Heavenly Father does have love toward every single person and calls us out of sin as we are. However, if we want to be treated and loved as sons and daughters, then we should treat Him and love Him as our Heavenly Father.

Mind you, there is a huge difference between a want and need. In response to our love and obedience toward Him, God provides for our needs, and He blesses us with our wants. Wants are not just handed over though, and unanswered prayers are inevitable. He is not trying to raise spiritually spoiled Christians, but rather patient, obedient Christians. We do have real needs and He knows them before we even ask.

"So do not be like them; for your Father knows what you need before you ask Him." (Matthew 6:8)

Parents do not simply hand over everything their children ask for just because they ask, right? They have to be sure it's not going to cause present or future harm. Parents have to see if the behavior is deserving of the request. They also ask, "What is my child going to do with this thing that they are asking for? Could it hurt them or someone else?" Our Father already knows the answer to these questions and responds accordingly.

There are questions we also should ask ourselves first before asking God for anything and then complaining when we don't receive it. Don't misunderstand, our Father is full of grace and mercy; He answers prayers, even when our actions may not be deserving. The Bible tells us that God's ear is open to all that call upon Him. He wants to help us, but He also knows our hearts and our intents. How many times has He come through for us when we least deserved it? Imagine what He will do when we are obedient to His ways. The whole Bible is full of examples of what God did for those that truly walked as His children in this world. His Word teaches us that those who fully follow Christ will be rewarded not just in this life but most importantly, with the ultimate reward of eternal life.

> *"Jesus said, Truly I say to you, there is no one who has left house or brothers or sisters or mother or father or children or farms, for My sake and for the gospel's sake, but that he will receive a hundred times as much now in the present age, houses and brothers and sisters and mothers and children and farms, along with persecutions; and in the age to come, eternal life."* (Mark 10:29-30)

It is my opinion that too many church-goers live the way they want and do whatever they want and still expect God's blessing in their lives. They expect to receive what they ask for in spite of their disobedience. We all know what happens when parents spoil their children. When a child is spoiled, what type of adult do they grow up to be? Maybe it's the friend who has a hard time coping when things don't go their way. Maybe it's the coworker who feels entitled to what other employees have without working hard. Or maybe it's the person who blames everyone else for their unhappiness. All hope is not lost for someone who was raised that way because God can change anyone's heart. It is just a bit harder because they have to learn to walk again—yes, I said walk again. When parents give their children everything they want, they are pulling their legs out from under them; it cripples them. We have to be taught money doesn't grow on trees and that things aren't going to be handed to us on a silver platter. We need reminding that we can't always do or get what we want just because we want it. One of the most valuable lessons is that we will not always win and we need to know what it is like to lose; we are better for it. When children aren't taught these valuable lessons, they are being set up for disappointment and failure. These children grow up to be adults who have a hard time adjusting to and coping with real life disappointments and losses. Their strength and endurance never matured; it never had to. Now they have to learn how to walk as they go instead of being better prepared for life beforehand. Our Heavenly Father does not want to spiritually cripple us, He wants to shape us into being spiritually strong, patient, and enduring Christians.

When we don't receive what we ask for, we have to ask ourselves two questions: Are we doing our best to live for God? If we truly are making a conscious effort to love and obey the Lord, then is what we want really what is best for us? Sometimes we know what we're asking for may not be good for us or someone else or the reason is not good, but we still ask.

> *"You ask and do not receive, because you ask with wrong motives, so that you may spend it on your pleasures."* (James 4:3)

Maybe it's just not the perfect time to receive what we are asking for and so we must learn to patiently wait. Do you remember asking your parents for something, hearing a yes, and feeling the excitement swell up in you? Then it was quickly deflated when you heard, "… but not right now." Oh, the suffering we endured as children! It was like, "Ughhh, why do I have to wait?!" Sometimes our parents were waiting for the right moment to give us what we were asking for. They thought it would make a better birthday gift. Maybe we asked in January and our birthday wasn't until June. So, it was a "no" until June when we received it for our birthday! Whatever the reason we don't receive what we ask for right away, our Heavenly Father knows best. Isn't it amazing to understand God's ways and how He works? A parent's love and concern for their child's well-being, both now and in the future, truly reflects that of God's love and concern for His children. He is our Heavenly Father and He wants to raise us right.

> *"'Therefore, come out from their midst and be separate,' says the Lord. 'And do not touch what is unclean; and I will welcome you. And I will be a father to you, and you shall be sons and daughters to Me', says the Lord Almighty." (2 Corinthians 6:17-18)*

3

I TOLD YOU

It's amazing how proud we humans can be sometimes. We think we're so smart. We think we know it all, and no one can tell us different. Does this sound like a younger version of ourselves? We thought we knew everything and had it all figured out, then our parents just had to go and prove us wrong. We heard the three infamous words, "I told you." Sometimes, I think God lets out a little chuckle when our heads start to swell and then He pops that balloon head of ours and brings us back to earth. We are mere mortals; our knowledge comes nowhere near to God's. Let's look at what He says about our way versus His way:

> *"Let the wicked forsake his way and the unrighteous man his thoughts; and let him return to the LORD, and He*

> *will have compassion on him, and to our God, for He will abundantly pardon.*
>
> *'For My thoughts are not your thoughts, nor are your ways My ways,' declares the LORD.*
>
> *'For as the heavens are higher than the earth, so are My ways higher than your ways and My thoughts than your thoughts.'"* (Isaiah 55:7-9)

The Lord is telling us that when we do things our way, because we think we know better, it causes us to separate from Him. He tells us to forsake our own way and our own thoughts and return to Him. Walking in our own way leads to sin and trouble, which is parallel to the mentality we had when we were young. "My parents said I can't go to a party with my friends, because they think my friends are trouble. But they always have parties and nothing happens to them. I'll be fine." A quote from the ever-smart, never-wrong, *young* person. So, we went without our parents knowing about it, and nothing happened to us. We had fun hanging out with our friends—doing things we shouldn't be doing but we weren't getting caught, so it was okay. We continued going back, thinking our parents were so wrong because nothing bad happened. In Ecclesiastes, God speaks of this very thing through King Solomon.

> *"Because the sentence against an evil deed is not executed quickly, therefore the hearts of the sons of men among them are given fully to do evil."* (Ecclesiastes 8:11)

We continued to be disobedient because there was no punishment for it at the time. Until one day, unexpectedly, the cops showed up and you were driven home in a police car. You were standing at your front door dreading the look on your dad's face when he opened the door. You knew he wouldn't punish you right away because a cop was present, but you cringed at the thought of what would happen after the cop left. You were then forced to sit at the kitchen table and explain why you deliberately disobeyed. "I told you, but you didn't listen! Now, look at what trouble you are in. It could have been much worse; you could have been hurt or even killed! That party wasn't a place for you to be at—I told you!" This is a Mayberry example (the town *The Andy Griffith Show* was based in, for those too young to know what Mayberry is). For some, scenarios similar to this don't end well or sadly, end up tragic. We think to ourselves, *If they had only listened, maybe things would have turned out differently.* The most important part of Isaiah 55:7-9 is that if the wicked and unrighteous man returns unto the Lord, then He will have compassion on him. He will not just pardon but *"abundantly pardon" (v. 7).* When we found ourselves in trouble, didn't we call our parents—even though we knew we would get into more trouble? Yes, and we either got scolded or comforted depending on our parents or the situation. In my home, it was more comfort with a gentle scolding from my mom and a firm scolding, coming from a place of concern, from my dad. Aren't we glad we serve a loving, merciful God who scolds us but also comforts us?

> *"And you have forgotten the exhortation which is addressed to you as sons, 'My son, do not regard lightly the discipline of the Lord, nor faint when you are reproved by Him; for those whom the Lord loves He disciplines, and He scourges every son whom He receives.' It is for discipline that you endure; God deals with you as with sons; for what son is there whom his father does not discipline? But if you are without discipline, of which all have become partakers, then*

> *you are illegitimate children and not sons. Furthermore, we had earthly fathers to discipline us, and we respected them; shall we not much rather be subject to the Father of spirits, and live? For they disciplined us for a short time as seemed best to them, but He disciplines us for our good, so that we may share His holiness."* (Hebrews 12:5-10)

Our Lord treats us just like a parent—parents can learn a lot from Him. When we are punished, it's not a joyous occasion, but it is for our betterment.

> *"The rod and reproof give wisdom, but a child who gets his own way brings shame to his mother."* (Proverbs 29:15)

> *"Correct your son, and he will give you comfort; he will also delight your soul."* (Proverbs 29:17)

> *"Foolishness is bound up in the heart of a child; the rod of discipline will remove it far from him."* (Proverbs 22:15)

If there is no correction or reproof, then foolishness remains, but when there is correction or reproof, it gives wisdom. Children will make mistakes just like we, as children of God, make mistakes. Even after we've been told not to do something, we still do it; but God has to correct us if we are going to be made wise and become more like Him.

I'm reminded of the recent Fruit Snack Challenge that was being posted all over social media. For those who are unaware, let me explain. Parents would open a bag of fruit snacks, put them in front of their kids, and walk away, but not before telling the kids that they could not touch nor eat the snacks until the parent returns. With cameras rolling, the parent walks away and observes the child's reactions. Seeing those kids struggle with themselves to not touch or eat the fruit snacks was quite a hilarious show. In all cases, the struggle was clear. Some of the children would talk out loud to themselves, reminding them of what their parent said. Others had to put the snacks out of sight, so not to struggle with the temptation. Some gave in, some almost gave in and then quickly retreat, and some patiently waited. Isn't this how we are with God sometimes? As adults, our struggles may not be evident to others, but our struggles—big or small—are always seen by God. We know what He said not to do, but we have this fleshly nature that we battle every day (and sometimes fail). Through the inspiration of the Holy Ghost, Paul describes this struggle best in Romans 7:18-25.

> *"For I know that nothing good dwells in me, that is, in my flesh; for the willing is present in me, but the doing of the good is not. For the good that I want, I do not do, but I practice the very evil that I do not want. But if I am doing the very thing I do not want, I am no longer the one doing it, but sin which dwells in me.*
>
> *I find then the principle that evil is present in me, the one who wants to do good. For I joyfully concur with the law of God in the inner man, but I see a different law in the members of my body, waging war against the law of my mind and making me a prisoner of the law of sin which is in my members. Wretched man that I am! Who will set me free from the body of this death? Thanks be to God through Jesus Christ our Lord! So then, on the one hand I myself with my mind am serving the law of God, but on the other, with my flesh the law of sin."*

Paul wasn't out there committing all kinds of sin or in bondage to sin. What he's saying is that no matter how much we desire to do right, we sometimes fail. Maybe unintentionally the wrong thing comes out of our mouth. Maybe we unknowingly offend someone. Or maybe wrong thoughts pop into our head. We fail, even if our whole heart and mind want to obey God.

Going back to the "Fruit Snack Challenge," all of the children got to eat the fruit snacks. Some did it out of disobedience, while others got to eat it after being obedient. What's the difference if we obey or not? What's the point of obedience if the righteous and the unrighteous both prosper in this life? The difference is that one is obedient and the other is not. Obedience will be rewarded in the end, when the great separation takes place between the righteous and the unrighteous. The unrighteous only get temporary satisfaction in this world, while the righteous receive rewards for obedience in this world and also in the world to come.

> *"Another parable He put forth to them, saying: 'The kingdom of heaven is like a man who sowed good seed in his field; but while men slept, his enemy came and sowed tares among the wheat and went his way. But when the grain had sprouted and produced a crop, then the tares also appeared. So the servants of the owner came and said to him, 'Sir, did you not sow good seed in your field? How then does it have tares?' He said to them, 'An enemy has done this.' The servants said to him, 'Do you want us then to go and gather them up?' But he said, 'No, lest while you gather up the tares you also uproot the wheat with them. Let both grow together until the harvest, and at the time of harvest I will say to the reapers, 'First gather together the tares and bind them in bundles to burn them, but gather the wheat into my barn.'"* (Matthew 13:24-30, NKJV)

Let us look for the bigger reward and not just the very temporary satisfactions this world has to offer. Let this be your reason to walk in obedience with our Heavenly Father as Paul said.

"I have fought the good fight, I have finished the course, I have kept the faith; in the future there is laid up for me the crown of righteousness, which the Lord, the righteous Judge, will award to me on that day; and not only to me, but also to all who have loved His appearing." (2 Timothy 4:7-8)

We can only love His appearing when we have confidence toward Him and are not ashamed because we've lived obedient lives. We don't want Him to tell us, "I told you" when we stand before Him at the great separation. Instead, we want to hear these words:

"Well done, good and faithful servant." (Matthew 25:23, KJV)

4

AN EMPATHETIC FATHER

Sometimes parents tell their children, "I know because I was your age once" or "I know, I went through the same thing when I was younger." Parents can relate to our growing pains because they were there once too. My mom used to always tell us, "You can tell me anything. Nothing is going to shock me or make me judge you. I know what it's like to be young, to make mistakes, and to do things you regret." This same relation, to a degree, can be made to our Heavenly Father. He never committed a sin, but He experienced the struggles we go through in this world, having walked the same earth as us. Yes, He has power and His Spirit fills the heavens and the earth, but that does not prevent Him from relating to us. In His human form, He was tempted just like we are. He was hated, mocked, and ridiculed by many. He felt pain, grief, and anger, yet never sinned. He experienced loss and loneliness. He endured all of these things and had His life taken away from Him at an early age, yet He overcame it all! We also can be victorious through Him.

Prayer was a necessity for our Lord Jesus Christ and crucial to His victory. He was strengthened through prayer. Just as parents pray for their children, God Himself prayed for us while He was on this earth—how powerful and amazing is that?

> *"But now I come to You; and these things I speak in the world so that they may have My joy made full in themselves. I have given them Your word; and the world has hated them, because they are not of the world, even as I am not of the world. I do not ask You to take them out of the world, but to keep them from the evil one. They are not of the world, even as I am not of the world. Sanctify them in the truth; Your word is truth. As You sent Me into the world, I also have sent them into the world. For their sakes I sanctify Myself, that they themselves also may be sanctified in truth. I do not ask on behalf of these alone, but for those also who believe in Me through their word; that they may all be one; even as You, Father, are in Me and I in You, that they also may be in Us, so that the world may believe that You sent Me."* (John 17:13-21)

> *"These things I have spoken to you, so that in Me you may have peace. In the world you have tribulation, but take courage; I have overcome the world."* (John 16:33)

> *"For we do not have a high priest who cannot sympathize with our weaknesses, but One who has been tempted in all things as we are, yet without sin."* (Hebrews 4:15)

The Scripture doesn't say He was incapable of sin, it says "without sin." The Lord Jesus Christ chose to be submissive to His Spirit at all times—never once giving into any temptation. In His humanity, He was physically capable of committing a sin. He could have hated Judas Iscariot, but instead, He called him friend the moment Judas betrayed Him. Jesus could have fought back when people mocked Him, called Him names, or lied about Him, but He didn't. The Lord Jesus Christ chose the way of His Spirit, not His flesh. He provided the perfect example of what it means to walk in the Spirit. But to walk in the Spirit, we need His help. We need His Holy Spirit in us.

> *"Therefore let us draw near with confidence to the throne of grace, so that we may receive mercy and find grace to help in time of need."* (Hebrews 4:16)

> *"For every high priest taken from among men is appointed on behalf of men in things pertaining to God, in order to offer both gifts and sacrifices for sins; he can deal gently with the ignorant and misguided, since he himself also is beset with weakness; and because of it he is obligated to offer sacrifices for sins, as for the people, so also for himself. And no one takes the honor to himself, but receives it when he is called by God, even as Aaron was. So also Christ did not glorify Himself so as to become a high priest, but He who said to Him, 'You are My Son, today I have begotten You'; just as He says also in another passage, 'You are a priest forever according to the order of Melchizedek.' In the days of His flesh, He offered up both prayers and supplications with loud crying and tears to the One able to save Him from death, and He was heard because of His piety. Although He was a Son, He learned obedience from the things which He suffered."* (Hebrews 5:1-8)

> *"For indeed He was crucified because of weakness, yet He lives because of the power of God. For we also are weak in*

Him, yet we will live with Him because of the power of God directed toward you." (2 Corinthians 13:4)

As a teenager, I remember listening to the testimony of Stephanie Fast and being moved to tears by all that she went through growing up as a homeless child in post-war Korea. The part that touched me the most was when she spoke about harboring anger toward all the people who had hurt her and tried to kill her. She felt like she had a right to be angry with them. Her father then tells her about Jesus. He explained how Jesus was betrayed, rejected, beaten, mocked, and even murdered. He told her that Jesus knew what she was going through because He had been there too. How comforting it is to know that we have a Heavenly Father who can relate to pain and suffering, but who has left us an example of forgiveness and overcoming. Our friends and family can sympathize, offering support and encouraging words for our pain and suffering, but only our Heavenly Father can empathize, knowing our pain and suffering firsthand.

5

THE TEACHER

An earthly father teaches his children morals and life skills. In order to teach his children God's ways, a father must be learning from his teacher—God. The Lord teaches His children His ways through His Word and through experiences. Although a mother can also teach her children the ways of God, teaching was never meant to be her responsibility alone. While teaching is a joint effort, the father bears the overall responsibility to bring his children up in the Lord and to have a household pleasing to God. Let's look at what God had to say about His friend, Abraham.

> *"For I have chosen him, so that he may command his children and his household after him to keep the way of the LORD by doing righteousness and justice, so that the LORD may bring upon Abraham what He has spoken about him."* (Genesis 18:19)

In order to command your children and household, you first have to teach them. Impart your knowledge of God and help them develop a relationship with the Lord until they're old enough to maintain that relationship themselves. Isaac learned about the promise and the things of God from Abraham, and Jacob learned it from Isaac. The list goes on and on from generation to generation of fathers teaching God's promises and commandments to their families.

Ephesians 6:4 was used earlier in reference to fear and respect. Read it again and pay close attention to who it is addressing in this Scripture.

"Fathers, do not provoke your children to anger, but bring them up in the discipline and instruction of the Lord." (Ephesians 6:4)

Fathers are supposed to instruct their children in the Lord. Instruction requires communication, which is crucial to effective teaching. Communication is not a one-way street. Our Father doesn't just talk to us; He listens while we talk to Him. We should feel like we can tell Him anything, just like we should be able to talk to our parents about anything. My parents always kept that line of communication open, making me feel that I could tell them anything—as hard as some things were to tell. I would receive spiritual advice and walk away feeling hopeful or knowing what to do. That's how God is with us because He knows what we are going through. He knows what we are feeling and thinking—right or wrong. He just wants to have an open and honest conversation with us, sincerely from the heart.

"Behold, You desire truth in the innermost being, and in the hidden part You will make me know wisdom." (Psalms 51:6)

"The LORD is near to all who call upon Him, to all who call upon Him in truth." (Psalms 145:18)

"'Come now, and let us reason together,' says the LORD, 'though your sins are as scarlet, they will be as white as snow; though they are red like crimson, they will be like wool.'" (Isaiah 1:18)

Leading by example is another key to effective teaching. God didn't just tell us His ways, He showed us when He manifested as Jesus Christ! He walked the walk. He was born into this world and lived in a body of flesh and blood as the ultimate example. Now we can look up to Him, just like a child looks up to their father. When a son looks up to his father, he wants to do everything his father does and wants to grow up to be just like him; no one is better or stronger than his father. A daughter looks up to her father as her defender and protector; her first love. Can we look at our Heavenly Father and feel the same way? Let's go through the following questions.

- Can we say that no one is stronger than our God?

    "O Lord GOD, You have begun to show Your servant Your greatness and Your strong hand; for what god is there in heaven or on earth who can do such works and mighty acts as Yours?" (Deuteronomy 3:24)

- Should we try to be like our Father?

    "Therefore be imitators of God, as beloved children." (Ephesians 5:1)

- Is He our defender and protector?

> *"I will lift up my eyes to the mountains; from where shall my help come? My help comes from the LORD, who made heaven and earth. He will not allow your foot to slip; He who keeps you will not slumber. Behold, He who keeps Israel will neither slumber nor sleep. The LORD is your keeper; the LORD is your shade on your right hand. The sun will not smite you by day, nor the moon by night. The LORD will protect you from all evil; He will keep your soul. The LORD will guard your going out and your coming in from this time forth and forever."* (Psalms 121:1-8)

- Most importantly, is He truly our first love?

> *"But I have this against you, that you have left your first love. Therefore remember from where you have fallen, and repent and do the deeds you did at first; or else I am coming to you and will remove your lampstand out of its place—unless you repent."* (Revelation 2:4-5)

> *"On my bed night after night I sought him whom my soul loves; I sought him but did not find him. 'I must arise now and go about the city; in the streets and in the squares I must seek him whom my soul loves.' I sought him but did not find him. "The watchmen who make the rounds in the city found me, and I said, 'Have you seen him whom my soul loves?' "Scarcely had I left them when I found him whom my soul loves; I held on to him and would not let him go until I had brought him to my mother's house, and into the room of her who conceived me."* (Song of Solomon 3:1-4)

If you don't feel this kind of connection with the Lord Jesus Christ, it's not too late to start developing a Father-child relationship with Him. This is not my idea of God, it is His. The way He shows Himself in His Word and deals with us in our lives proves His desire for relationship. Ask Him to help you love Him this way. I still ask Him to help me love Him more. A lot of times when a child is adopted, they don't automatically love their parents the way a child who is born to their parents loves them. Stephanie Fast also testifies to this as she was eventually adopted. She had to learn to feel and show that kind of love to her adoptive parents. That relationship is a process and takes time to develop. It's the same with the Lord Jesus Christ. He adopts us and becomes our Heavenly Father, but we bring along pain, hurt and sometimes damage from life experiences. In spite of it all, He is the good Father who helps us heal and teaches us His ways to build and grow our relationship with Him. He ultimately wants our hearts.

> *"Give me your heart, my son, and let your eyes delight in my ways."* (Proverbs 23:26)

> *"For all who are being led by the Spirit of God, these are sons of God. For you have not received a spirit of slavery leading to fear again, but you have received a spirit of adoption as sons by which we cry out, 'Abba! Father!' The Spirit Himself testifies with our spirit that we are children of God."* (Romans 8:14-16)

> *"Because you are sons, God has sent forth the Spirit of His Son into our hearts, crying, 'Abba! Father!'"* (Galatians 4:6)

> *"See how great a love the Father has bestowed on us, that we would be called children of God; and such we are. For this reason the world does not know us, because it did not know Him."* (1 John 3:1)

How does He teach us? He teaches us through His Word. It is the Word of God that leads us, guides us, directs our path, and tells us right from wrong. Psalms

119:105 says, *"Your word is a lamp to my feet and a light to my path."* The more we live by God's Word, the more we are exercised through it, and the closer we become to mature, strong Christians.

> *"For everyone who partakes only of milk is not accustomed to the word of righteousness, for he is an infant. But solid food is for the mature, who because of practice have their senses trained to discern good and evil."* (Hebrews 5:13-14)

A FATHER WE CAN TRUST

Some people get bitter toward God when unfortunate events happen. Maybe God is trying to get their attention because they've been stubborn all this time or maybe there is an unforeseen reason for the unfortunate event that only He knows. Whatever the reason, we have to get to a point where we love God and respect His ways because they are not our ways. Father knows best, right? When we can't accept that, it's because we still feel like we know best. We have to learn to let go of our own understanding and trust God's ways. Once we realized our parents were right, we stopped testing them and instead began to trust them. Same goes for our relationship with our Heavenly Father. When we begin to believe Him, that He is all-knowing, just, and righteous in all things, then we can begin to trust Him.

> *"Trust in the LORD with all your heart and do not lean on your own understanding. In all your ways acknowledge Him, and He will make your paths straight. Do not be wise in your own eyes; fear the LORD and turn away from evil. It will be healing to your body and refreshment to your bones."* (Proverbs 3:5-8)

Verse 7 could be read like this: Do not be wise in your own eyes, respect the Lord and depart from evil. When we have a hard time trusting God, it's because we're doubting what He has told us. We feel like we can figure it out for ourselves. Many times, this leads to trouble and we find ourselves in need of God's help because we didn't trust Him from the beginning. The verse is saying that fearing the Lord and turning away from evil is what is healing and refreshing to your body. In other words, trusting God is for your own health and well-being.

As children, we were stubborn in our ways and became even more stubborn as adults. God sees stubbornness in adults the same as He sees iniquity and idolatry, and rebellion the same as witchcraft. He made this known to King Saul through the prophet Samuel when King Saul would not obey God.

> *"For rebellion is as the sin of divination, and insubordination is as iniquity and idolatry. Because you have rejected the word of the LORD, He has also rejected you from being king."* (1 Samuel 15:23)

Why iniquity, idolatry, and divination (or witchcraft) specifically? Well, iniquity is immorality and so insubordination (or stubbornness) is not accepting the standards of morality—what is right and wrong. Idolatry is the worship of and service to anything other than God. When we are full of our own ways, we are serving ourselves, worshipping ourselves, and thinking we know better than God. In God's eyes, rebellion is as reprehensible as the sin of witchcraft. When we rebel against the Lord, we are rejecting His Word. In the same way, people reject God by inquiring of witchcraft or divination for guidance or counsel. Rebellion is the sin of Satan. He rebelled and he tries to make us rebel as well. King Saul thought he could stubbornly rebel and God would be pleased with his sacrifices; however, as we read in 1 Samuel 15:23, the Lord rejected him. Let's not deceive ourselves with good works or sacrifices. We are either in obedience or we are in stubbornness and rebellion.

> *"Does the Lord have as much delight in burnt offerings and sacrifices as in obeying the voice of the Lord? Behold, to obey is better than a sacrifice, and to pay attention is better than the fat of rams.* (1 Samuel 15:22)

As Proverbs 28:26 says, *"He who trusts in his own heart is a fool, but he who walks wisely will be delivered."* We don't want to be fools; we want to walk wisely. Trusting in ourselves is considered foolish. If we're walking wisely, we will escape the things that come to those who walk according to their own heart. This doesn't mean that absolutely nothing will ever go wrong or that we will never get hurt. Children get hurt; adults get hurt—hurt is inevitable. We all fell while riding our bikes or maybe tripped while running. Even now, God tells us to watch our step, yet we still fall. As long as we are in this world, we will get hurt. But like our parents helped clean the wound and comforted us, the Lord Jesus does the same for us now. We didn't trust our parents any less because we tripped and fell on their watch. In this life, pain is guaranteed because of evil, but God can use our pain to bring us closer to Him, if we allow it. He never said we will not go through hard times, but He did promise to be there for us when we do.

Our God wants us to call upon Him as our Father, whom we trust to be with us and guide us throughout our lives.

> *"Will you not from this time cry to Me, 'My Father, You are the guide of my youth?"* (Jeremiah 3:4, NKJV)

Youth is a critical stage where lessons are taught that help form mature adults. I read "the guide of my youth" as the guide of my critical learning stage. Our Heavenly Father is teaching and guiding us in our spiritual youth so that we can learn to trust Him completely and reach spiritual maturity.

7

A GRIEVED FATHER

God longs to guide us with a Fatherly love. It is we, as rebellious children, who are persistent to go our own way and find ourselves separated from our Father.

> *"All of us like sheep have gone astray, each of us has turned to his own way; but the LORD has caused the iniquity of us all to fall on Him."* (Isaiah 53:6)

> *"Jerusalem, Jerusalem, who kills the prophets and stones those who are sent to her! How often I wanted to gather your children together, the way a hen gathers her chicks under her wings, and you were unwilling."* (Matthew 23:37)

Our rebellious ways can grieve God just like a son or daughter can cause a parent grief. The last thing a parent wants is for their child to live a reckless, rebellious life, going against the laws of the land and going against everything that is right. It grieves parents to see their children in jail or become drug addicts, alcoholics, murderers, or even just to see them not do anything with their lives. I've seen the grief that sons and daughters can cause a parent. Shamefully, I've been part of the reason for that grief. You always hear parents say, "They weren't raised that way," when referring to something their son or daughter did wrong.

I'm reminded of an experience that one of my nieces, who was eleven at the time, had with a boy from school. He had been giving her some trouble on the bus and while walking the short distance home. My sister and my parents tried to handle the situation without talking to his parents; however, one day, he gave my niece a vulgar, unpleasant letter on the bus, calling her names. My mom decided to take that letter to his house and let his parents know what was going on. She spoke with his father, and he said he would take care of it. About 20 minutes later, his father showed up to my parents' house with his son. He brought his son over so he could personally apologize to my niece. I'll never forget, this father had his son get on his knees while tearfully begging my niece for forgiveness. His father said, "I did not raise my son to talk that way, and we definitely don't treat women or girls that way. I don't know where he got that from, but I apologize and I promise you it won't happen again." My niece never had an issue with the boy again. That boy learned a valuable lesson that day. Even though he didn't learn that behavior from his father, it took his father addressing the issue in order for a change to take place. This is reflective of our Father's way; He didn't teach us to do wrong, but rebellion is set in our hearts and it must be dealt with in order for us to change. We have to be humbled as this young boy was. God tried for 40 years to teach the children of Israel to do right, but they were stubborn. They did not trust God, so they did what they wanted to do instead.

> *"Therefore, just as the Holy Spirit says, 'Today if you hear His voice, do not harden your hearts as when they provoked Me, as in the day of trial in the wilderness, where your fathers tried Me by testing Me, and saw My works for forty years. Therefore I was angry with this generation, and said, "They always go astray in their heart, and they did not know My ways."'"* (Hebrews 3:7-10)

So, here's a question: Were the children of Israel, who disobeyed, punished? Oh yes, they were, many times! There is no justification to being upset when we are punished for doing wrong. God, as our Father, gave parents the perfect example of punishment throughout His Word. What is the part of punishment that often gets left out? Talking. God always told His people *what* they were doing wrong and *why* they were being punished. He would send the prophets to warn the people over and over or to tell them they were going to be punished. Sometimes, He would even change His mind based on His people's response and not go through with the punishment. He had compassion on His people. I remember getting away with a few spankings in my youth simply because I melted my dad's heart with something I said or did, such as raise my hand to receive the first spanking. I obviously didn't understand what I was asking for at such a young age, but I think my dad was reminded of my innocence—that I didn't intentionally set out to do something wrong. He remembered that I was a child still learning the difference between right and wrong, and he wasn't able to go through with the punishment.

Even though we can cause grief in our lifetime, our Father is ready to pardon us and receive us again when we come to Him in true repentance. He wants us to turn away from our wrongdoings and change as He tells us in Ezekiel 18:27-32.

> *"Again, when a wicked man turns away from his wickedness which he has committed and practices justice and righteousness, he will save his life. Because he considered and turned away from all his transgressions which he had committed, he shall surely live; he shall not die. But the house of Israel says, 'The way of the Lord is not right.' Are My ways not right, O house of Israel? Is it not your ways that are not right?*
>
> *'Therefore I will judge you, O house of Israel, each according to his conduct,' declares the Lord GOD. 'Repent and turn away from all your transgressions, so that iniquity may not become a stumbling block to you. Cast away from you all your transgressions which you have committed and make yourselves a new heart and a new spirit! For why will you die, O house of Israel? For I have no pleasure in the death of anyone who dies,' declares the Lord GOD. 'Therefore, repent and live.'"*

He knows we fail, but He doesn't want us just going in circles like the children of Israel. They grieved Him because they couldn't understand His ways and constantly failed. Sadly, all but two who were delivered from the bondage of Egypt fell short of the promised land. We must learn, grow, and mature spiritually so we don't grieve our Heavenly Father.

> *"Do not grieve the Holy Spirit of God, by whom you were sealed for the day of redemption."* (Ephesians 4:30)

8
THE PERFECT FATHER

Not every person can say they have great parents or that their parents raised them right because parents make mistakes. My parents weren't perfect, but they did their best raising us. That's one difference between our earthly parents and our Heavenly Father—He makes no mistakes.

He always loves His children. He may not love what we do, but He always loves us and wants us to come to Him. He has compassion on us, but as I said before, He also gets hurt or is grieved by the things we do sometimes. He punishes when necessary to teach us right from wrong and to help us stay on the right path. He wants to raise children that will bring Him joy, not heartache and grief:

> *"A wise son makes a father glad, but a foolish son is a grief to his mother."* (Proverbs 10:1)

If someone grew up with abusive, neglectful parents, then we can't compare the way they were brought up to the way we are brought up by our Heavenly Father. Sadly, their parents' ways were not in line with God's ways. Peace and joy can still be brought to their life by knowing who our perfect Father is. He has kept them to this day, and wants to demonstrate the true love a parent should have for their child.

Some people are angry with God because He allowed them to go through abuse and torment as a child. I don't have all the answers or know what to say other than nothing was their fault as a child. In this world, the innocent one is always preyed upon by the person who does evil. Our Heavenly Father can relate even more than anyone else because He knows what it is like to be hated for no reason. He knows how it feels to be senselessly beaten and to suffer the most horrific death known to mankind. He knows what it feels like to be treated as if you don't matter; to be treated inhumanely. All of the forces of evil were unleashed on the Lord Jesus Christ to destroy Him (so they thought), while being an innocent man.

As long as evil exists in this world and people choose to live outside of God's ways, the innocent will suffer and be victimized. The devil's main objectives are to kill, steal, and destroy. He has no sympathy for innocent children. In fact, the devil preys on them now, more than ever before. He wants the cycle of evil to continue, and what better time to try to destroy us than while we are young and vulnerable? In the devil's perfect plan, we will carry the effects of trauma into adulthood; maybe ruin our lives or other people's lives along the way. He would love a world full of depressed, bitter, angry, heartless, and evil people. But the light of the

Lord Jesus Christ shines brighter than the darkness, and He came to destroy the works of the devil in the life of those who come to Him.

> *"The Son of God appeared for this purpose, to destroy the works of the devil."* (1 John 3:8b)

That's the raging battle between good and evil taking place all around us. God sees and knows all; He will judge accordingly and have compassion on the innocent. All we can do is trust our Father through the good and bad times. In the book of Job, we learn about a man whose faith was tested in some of the hardest ways you can imagine.

> *"There was a man in the land of Uz whose name was Job; and that man was blameless, upright, fearing God and turning away from evil.*
> *Seven sons and three daughters were born to him.*
> *His possessions also were 7,000 sheep, 3,000 camels, 500 yoke of oxen, 500 female donkeys, and very many servants; and that man was the greatest of all the men of the east."* (Job 1:1-3)

He was "the greatest of all the men of the east." So, what happened to this great man who served God and had everything going for him? Well, if you read on in Job, you'll learn that the devil thought Job was only serving God because God was making everything great for Job. Satan felt that God wasn't letting anything bad happen to Job and God was just blessing him left and right, so of course Job was faithful. God told Satan that he could touch whatever Job had, but he was to leave Job, himself, alone. So, the devil went to work. Job's oxen and donkeys were stolen, his sheep were killed in a fire, his camels were stolen, all of the servants in charge of those animals were killed, and his own sons were killed when the house they were in collapsed on them. Losing all of his animals and servants was tragic, but losing his sons must have been the worst of it all for Job. On top of the grief at the loss of his sons, the reality of not having anyone to carry on the family name and traditions was a huge deal in Job's day. The lineage that would carry his name and the knowledge of God for generations had been completely wiped out. Remember, Job had done nothing wrong to be given that much grief and suffer all of those losses. His righteousness remained through it all, and he continued to serve God in spite of what he had endured.

Did proving the devil wrong mean that everything just got better for Job after that? Nope. Satan still thought God was protecting Job too much and suggested that if God allowed Job to be afflicted, then Job would surely curse God to His face. So, God agreed, but Satan could not take Job's life. Satan went to work again and struck Job with boils from head to toe. It was so bad that his friends didn't even recognize him. In fact, they cried out loud when they saw him. Job's wife even encouraged Job in Job 2:9 to, "*Curse God and die!*" This was Job's response:

> "*But he said to her, 'You speak as one of the foolish women speaks. Shall we indeed accept good from God and not accept adversity?' In all this Job did not sin with his lips.*" (Job 2:10)

Most people would have been angry with God at that point. Some might even question how God could let all those things happen when we had done nothing wrong? All the while, it was Satan trying to prove his point and we end up being hurt. Sometimes, God has to let our hand go and see if we can walk on our own so to speak—not that we are alone but it feels like we are. God had to risk letting go of Job's hand in order for Job to be able to prove his faithfulness to Him.

Maybe our Father wants to prove that no matter how much evil and pain the devil brings upon us, that we will still choose Him in the end. Maybe, just maybe, our Father is like any parent who sends their young adult into the big world, praying that they will stay true to the values and ways they taught them. They will never know unless they let them go. In some cases, the Lord gives us examples in His Word of why things happen and how we all can learn His ways.

As hard as growing up may have been for some, as adults, we can no longer blame our parents for who we are or the condition we find ourselves in. As adults, we are able to make decisions on our own and make choices that determine our future. We now carry the responsibility to change and to choose how we are going to walk in this world—in our family's sins or in the way our Heavenly Father taught us in His Word.

> *"For this is the love of God, that we keep His commandments; and His commandments are not burdensome."* (1 John 5:3)

If we love our Heavenly Father, then we will keep His commandments. We will understand that no matter what happens, our Father is still perfect and doesn't make mistakes.

9

A SAVING FATHER

As we grow into adulthood, our parents stand by watching, hoping, and praying that everything they did for us (the blood, sweat and tears) will pay off. But what happens in most cases? Once we taste freedom as a young adult, we run with it! Some longer and harder than others. The perfect example of how we do this to our Heavenly Father is told by our Father Himself in the parable of the prodigal son:

"And He said, A man had two sons.

The younger of them said to his father, 'Father, give me the share of the estate that falls to me.' So he divided his wealth between them. And not many days later, the younger son gathered everything together and went on a journey into a distant country, and there he squandered his estate with loose living.

Now when he had spent everything, a severe famine occurred in that country, and he began to be impoverished. So he went and hired himself out to one of the citizens of that country, and he sent him into his fields to feed swine. And he would have gladly filled his stomach with the pods that the swine were eating, and no one was giving anything to him. But when he came to his senses, he said, 'How many of my father's hired men have more than enough bread, but I am dying here with hunger! I will get up and go to my father, and will say to him, "Father, I have sinned against heaven, and in your sight; I am no longer worthy to be called your son; make me as one of your hired men.' So he got up and came to his father. But while he was still a long way off, his father saw him and felt compassion for him, and ran and embraced him and kissed him. And the son said to him, 'Father, I have sinned against heaven and in your sight; I am no longer worthy to be called your son.' But the father said to his slaves, 'Quickly bring out the best robe and put it on him, and put a ring on his hand and sandals on his feet; and bring the fattened calf, kill it, and let us eat and celebrate; for this son of mine was dead and has come to life again; he was lost and has been found.' And they began to celebrate.

Now his older son was in the field, and when he came and approached the house, he heard music and dancing. And he summoned one of the servants and began inquiring what these things could be. And he said to him, 'Your brother has come, and your father has killed the fattened calf because he has received him back safe and sound.' But he became angry and was not willing to go in; and his father came out and began pleading with him. But he answered and said to his father, 'Look! For so many years I have been serving you and I have never neglected a command of yours; and yet you have never given me a young goat, so that I might celebrate with my friends; but when this son of yours came, who has devoured your wealth with prostitutes, you killed the fattened calf for him.'

> *And he said to him, 'Son, you have always been with me, and all that is mine is yours. But we had to celebrate and rejoice, for this brother of yours was dead and has begun to live, and was lost and has been found.'"* (Luke 15:11-32)

As Christians, sometimes we receive every good thing God can give us, yet we still go astray. I'm definitely guilty of that. What happens to us though? Like the prodigal son, we remember what we had when we walked in God's ways, and we long to come back in repentance because we know we let our Father down. What is so amazing is that the father in this parable was so happy to have his son back, there was no anger in his heart! Imagine you're on your knees crying in sorrow and regret for wasting everything your father has ever given you and because you've brought shame to your family. Now you're ready to make things right, so you look through your tears to see your dad running toward you. He can hardly wait to put his arms around you, so he's running with his arms held out, tears of joy falling from His eyes. He reaches for you, picks you up from the ground and embraces you like you did nothing wrong; like a father who's just beyond happy to have his child back. That's the Lord Jesus Christ, our Heavenly Father!

Back in the Old Testament, punishment was handed down over and over again to a rebellious people. I probably would not have survived the wilderness experience that's for sure. Thank God for the dispensation of grace! The Word tells us that all those things happened to them as an example for us now.

> *"For I do not want you to be unaware, brethren, that our fathers were all under the cloud and all passed through the sea; and all were baptized into Moses in the cloud and in the sea; and all ate the same spiritual food; and all*

drank the same spiritual drink, for they were drinking from a spiritual rock which followed them; and the rock was Christ. Nevertheless, with most of them God was not well-pleased; for they were laid low in the wilderness.

Now these things happened as examples for us, so that we would not crave evil things as they also craved. Do not be idolaters, as some of them were; as it is written, 'The people sat down to eat and drink, and stood up to play.' Nor let us act immorally, as some of them did, and twenty-three thousand fell in one day. Nor let us try the Lord, as some of them did, and were destroyed by the serpents. Nor grumble, as some of them did, and were destroyed by the destroyer. Now these things happened to them as an example, and they were written for our instruction, upon whom the ends of the ages have come. Therefore let him who thinks he stands take heed that he does not fall. No temptation has overtaken you but such as is common to man; and God is faithful, who will not allow you to be tempted beyond what you are able, but with the temptation will provide the way of escape also, so that you will be able to endure it." (1 Corinthians 10:1-13)

Most parents agree that there is nothing they wouldn't do to save their son or daughter. That's exactly how our Father felt. We all needed saving from sin, so what did He do for us? He gave the most anyone could ever give—Himself! The children of Israel gave sacrifices to God to atone for their sins, but it was basically the animal's life for their life. All of those sacrifices never removed their sins. God just chose to overlook their sin, but the shame and guilt remained. Hebrews 10:1-4 says:

"For the Law, since it has only a shadow of the good things to come and not the very form of things, can never, by the same sacrifices which they offer continually year by year, make perfect those who draw near. Otherwise, would they not have ceased to be offered, because the worshipers, having

once been cleansed, would no longer have had consciousness of sins? But in those sacrifices there is a reminder of sins year by year. For it is impossible for the blood of bulls and goats to take away sins."

In His foreknowledge, Our Father knew that after the fall of mankind, we would need saving. He knew that our carnal nature and sinful tendencies would be too much for us to handle on our own, so He had already prepared Himself to come save us. He had to let things play out though because He doesn't force us to come to Him. He knew the choices His people would make, even as much as He tried to teach us in the beginning. He had to let those be lessons for us now, as I mentioned previously. In continuation, the verse above talks about the body He prepared for us.

"Therefore, when He comes into the world, He says, 'Sacrifice and offering You have not desired, but a body You have prepared for Me; in whole burnt offerings and sacrifices for sin You have taken no pleasure. Then I said, 'Behold, I have come (In the scroll of the book it is written of Me) to do Your will, O God.' After saying above, 'Sacrifices and offerings and whole burnt offerings and sacrifices for sin You have not desired, nor have You taken pleasure in them' (which are offered according to the Law), then He said, 'Behold, I have come to do Your will.' He takes away the first in order to establish the second. By this will we have been sanctified through the offering of the body of Jesus Christ once for all. Every priest stands daily ministering and offering time after time the same sacrifices, which can never take away sins; but He, having offered one sacrifice for sins for all time, sat down at the right hand of God, waiting from that time onward until His enemies be made a footstool for His feet. For by one offering He has perfected for all time those who are sanctified." (Hebrews 10:5-14)

He prepared Himself to be the ultimate sacrifice, once and for all!

> *"Nor was it that He would offer Himself often, as the high priest enters the holy place year by year with blood that is not his own.*
>
> *Otherwise, He would have needed to suffer often since the foundation of the world; but now once at the consummation of the ages He has been manifested to put away sin by the sacrifice of Himself. And inasmuch as it is appointed for men to die once and after this comes judgment, so Christ also, having been offered once to bear the sins of many, will appear a second time for salvation without reference to sin, to those who eagerly await Him."* (Hebrews 9:25-28)

> *"And not through the blood of goats and calves, but through His own blood, He entered the holy place once for all, having obtained eternal redemption. For if the blood of goats and bulls and the ashes of a heifer sprinkling those who have been defiled sanctify for the cleansing of the flesh, how much more will the blood of Christ, who through the eternal Spirit offered Himself without blemish to God, cleanse your conscience from dead works to serve the living God?"* (Hebrews 9:12-14)

Our Father did it out of love. He came to the earth He created to lay down His life for us.

> *"We know love by this, that He laid down His life for us; and we ought to lay down our lives for the brethren."* (1 John 3:16)

> *"For God so loved the world, that He gave His only begotten Son, that whoever believes in Him shall not perish, but have eternal life."* (John 3:16)

Sadly, not everyone—then or now—accepted this ultimate sacrifice in their own lives. He was rejected by His own then, and He is rejected even now.

"There was the true Light which, coming into the world, enlightens every man. He was in the world, and the world was made through Him, and the world did not know Him. He came to His own, and those who were His own did not receive Him." (John 1:9-11)

The only reason we can be completely cleansed and forgiven of our sins is because our Heavenly Father, Jesus Christ, died for us. He sacrificed Himself for us so that we would not have to pay the price for our sins. No matter what we have done wrong, we can be cleansed. We can come to our Father and start over again.

Some parents have lost their lives trying to save their children from death. Sadly, if the children survive, they no longer have their parents. When our Father died, it did not end there. He raised Himself from the dead. He came back to life because He promised more than once that He would never leave us, nor forsake us.

"I will not leave you as orphans; I will come to you." (John 14:18)

"Teaching them to observe all that I commanded you; and lo, I am with you always, even to the end of the age." (Matthew 28:20)

"Make sure that your character is free from the love of money, being content with what you have; for He Himself has said, "I will never desert you, nor will I ever forsake you." (Hebrews 13:5)

> *"Be strong and courageous, do not be afraid or tremble at them, for the LORD your God is the one who goes with you. He will not fail you or forsake you."* (Deuteronomy 31:6)

Our Father's sacrifice now allows us to be completely cleansed from sin, even in our conscience. We can be found not guilty on judgement day because we have been cleansed through baptism.

> *"For Christ also died for sins once for all, the just for the unjust, so that He might bring us to God, having been put to death in the flesh, but made alive in the spirit; in which also He went and made proclamation to the spirits now in prison, who once were disobedient, when the patience of God kept waiting in the days of Noah, during the construction of the ark, in which a few, that is, eight persons, were brought safely through the water. Corresponding to that, baptism now saves you—not the removal of dirt from the flesh, but an appeal to God for a good conscience—through the resurrection of Jesus Christ, who is at the right hand of God, having gone into heaven, after angels and authorities and powers had been subjected to Him."* (1 Peter 3:18-22)

This is where the washing away of sins comes from—the cleansed conscience. Baptism is the burial of our body of sin, to come up out of the water forgiven, and receive salvation for our souls.

> *"Having been buried with Him in baptism, in which you were also raised up with Him through faith in the working of God, who raised Him from the dead. When you were dead in your transgressions and the uncircumcision of your flesh, He made you alive together with Him, having forgiven us all our transgressions;"* (Colossians 2:12-13)

"What shall we say then? Are we to continue in sin so that grace may increase? May it never be! How shall we who died to sin still live in it? Or do you not know that all of us who have been baptized into Christ Jesus have been baptized into His death? Therefore we have been buried with Him through baptism into death, so that as Christ was raised from the dead through the glory of the Father, so we too might walk in newness of life. For if we have become united with Him in the likeness of His death, certainly we shall also be in the likeness of His resurrection, knowing this, that our old self was crucified with Him, in order that our body of sin might be done away with, so that we would no longer be slaves to sin; for he who has died is freed from sin.

Now if we have died with Christ, we believe that we shall also live with Him, knowing that Christ, having been raised from the dead, is never to die again; death no longer is master over Him.

For the death that He died, He died to sin once for all; but the life that He lives, He lives to God. Even so consider yourselves to be dead to sin, but alive to God in Christ Jesus." (Romans 6:1-11)

According to the Scriptures, it is through baptism that we receive and accept the sacrifice our Heavenly Father paid for us. Not only to receive it but to remain in it, so that we do not go back to serving sin. As we continue reading from the Scripture above, Paul goes on to say:

"Therefore do not let sin reign in your mortal body so that you obey its lusts, and do not go on presenting the members of your body to sin as instruments of unrighteousness; but present yourselves to God as those alive from the dead, and your members as instruments of righteousness to God." (Romans 6:12-13)

> *"Giving thanks to the Father, who has qualified us to share in the inheritance of the saints in Light.*
>
> *For He rescued us from the domain of darkness, and transferred us to the kingdom of His beloved Son, in whom we have redemption, the forgiveness of sins.*
>
> *He is the image of the invisible God, the firstborn of all creation.*
>
> *For by Him all things were created, both in the heavens and on earth, visible and invisible, whether thrones or dominions or rulers or authorities—all things have been created through Him and for Him. He is before all things, and in Him all things hold together. He is also head of the body, the church; and He is the beginning, the firstborn from the dead, so that He Himself will come to have first place in everything. For it was the Father's good pleasure for all the fullness to dwell in Him, and through Him to reconcile all things to Himself, having made peace through the blood of His cross; through Him, I say, whether things on earth or things in heaven.*
>
> *And although you were formerly alienated and hostile in mind, engaged in evil deeds, yet He has now reconciled you in His fleshly body through death, in order to present you before Him holy and blameless and beyond reproach— if indeed you continue in the faith firmly established and steadfast, and not moved away from the hope of the gospel that you have heard, which was proclaimed in all creation under heaven, and of which I, Paul, was made a minister."*
> (Colossians 1:12-23)

I can't think of one gift my parents gave me that I rejected, yet the gift the Lord Jesus Christ gave us is, sadly, rejected by many. Some may receive it but then misuse it. This next application has no real comparison to the gift the Lord gave us, but please bear with me. A parent may give their child a gift like a game console, but then they have to take it away because their child spends too much time on it. The child abused something that was meant for good. When we misuse and abuse the gift that our Father gave us, we risk losing it for good.

> *"Anyone who has set aside the Law of Moses dies without mercy on the testimony of two or three witnesses. How much severer punishment do you think he will deserve who has trampled under foot the Son of God, and has regarded as unclean the blood of the covenant by which he was sanctified, and has insulted the Spirit of grace?"* (Hebrews 10:28-29)

Only God knows our hearts and knows the measure of grace each of us receives. Not that our hearts are good in and of themselves, but He knows where our hearts will lead us. Though some of us may find ourselves in a condition far from Him, He knows we will repent and return to Him—like the prodigal son. Other hearts, completely and totally turn away from God, and, unfortunately, they are the ones that never return.

> *"For in the case of those who have once been enlightened and have tasted of the heavenly gift and have been made partakers of the Holy Spirit, and have tasted the good word of God and the powers of the age to come, and then have fallen away, it is impossible to renew them again to repentance, since they again crucify to themselves the Son of God and put Him to open shame."* (Hebrews 6:4-6)

This is why it is extremely important we do not take our salvation lightly, nor take sin lightly in our lives. The Lord wants us to accept the gift that He gave unto us and paid for with His own body and to abide in it all the days of our lives.

OUR FATHER'S LOVE

Most Christians never truly understand or comprehend the height or depths of our Father's love. Everyone looks to the cross, which is the ultimate gift of love, but the love of Christ is also displayed when He fights for us. He will still go out and find us at our lowest point, when we can't find our way out of the rebellious state we put ourselves in. He leaves the 99 sheep to rescue the one—me and you. I wouldn't be where I am today if He hadn't rescued me.

If He were a neglectful Father, then there are a lot of us who would not have been rescued from sin. Instead, He is an attentive Father who fights and tears down; He goes as far as necessary in order to draw us to Him. The song, *"Reckless Love"* by Cory Asbury beautifully describes the depths and heights God's love will go to save His children. It's not that God is reckless. His love just seems reckless when we look at how much He has done and is willing to do to save us. He could have just left me for good, but He fought for me. Even when I pushed Him away, He still kept coming. No one could ever love us as our Heavenly Father does.

> *"The LORD appeared to him from afar, saying, 'I have loved you with an everlasting love; therefore I have drawn you with lovingkindness.'"* (Jeremiah 31:3)

Everyone born into this world needs saving, with the exception of our Father, the Lord Jesus Christ. As children, we don't know right from wrong, which is why we have to be taught. Once our conscience has developed and we have an understanding of what is right and wrong, then we are aware of our wrongdoings (sin). As the Lord said through the apostle Paul in Romans 7:9, sin becomes alive in us.

> *"I was once alive apart from the Law; but when the commandment came, sin became alive and I died."*

From the point that sin becomes alive in us, we need spiritual saving—not just being cleansed from sin. Our Father wants us to turn away from sin, to no longer choose what is wrong. Once we are rescued, we are to no longer get tangled up again in sin. Our parents don't ever want to bail us out of jail, but they will … the first time at least. They definitely don't want it to become a reoccurring issue. We should learn from our mistakes and not repeat them. Unfortunately, some of us take longer to learn than others.

Maybe you've seen or experienced this scenario: You're at the store and there's a toddler on the floor, crying and screaming at the top of their lungs. The child is upset because they're not getting whatever it is they want. Then the parent gives the child what they want in an effort to keep them quiet. I get it, it's an embarrassing disturbance, so the parent is trying to defuse the situation. But doesn't that teach the child that they can misbehave and still get what they want? Just as a child who acts out and misbehaves should not receive any rewards, we as God's children should not expect to receive anything while we are in a state of disobedience. However, a lot of times, compassion is what makes a parent give in even when a child doesn't deserve something. Parents feel bad for their child and don't want to make them cry. That is what makes our Heavenly Father even more loveable. This world was in such a state of disobedience when He brought the free gift of salvation into it. This gift was given because of God's mercy and compassion, not so much because He doesn't want us to cry so to speak. More importantly, He doesn't want us to die eternally because of our disobedience. He's not looking at our current feelings, but rather the long-term effect it will have on us. He brought us salvation not so that we can continue in our disobedience, but rather so that we can turn away from it and turn to Him.

Sometimes, He has to stop giving or take things away in order for us to change. Think about a parent who is trying to help their son or daughter with addiction. You can't give an addict everything they want. As much as it hurts, sometimes, the best thing a parent can do is say no. And sometimes we have to hit rock bottom and lose everything in order to realize the error of our ways and turn our lives around. It doesn't seem like love, but it is. This is the same tough love our Heavenly Father demonstrates to us. Thankfully, He is very patient, gracious, and merciful. So how does He initially free us from sin once we become aware of it? Let's read what Jesus said in Luke 24:46-47 (NKJV):

> *"Then He said to them, 'Thus it is written, and thus it was necessary for the Christ to suffer and to rise from the dead the third day, and that repentance and remission of sins should be preached in His name to all nations, beginning at Jerusalem.'"*

Repentance is to turn away from sin; remission is the complete removal or forgiveness of our sins. How is this done in His name? There are several Scriptures that answer this question.

> *"And he said, 'The God of our fathers has appointed you to know His will and to see the Righteous One and to hear an utterance from His mouth. For you will be a witness for Him to all men of what you have seen and heard. Now why do you delay? Get up and be baptized, and wash away your sins, calling on His name.'"* (Acts 22:14-16)

> *"But when they believed Philip preaching the good news about the kingdom of God and the name of Jesus Christ, they were being baptized, men and women alike."* (Acts 8:12)

> *"And there is salvation in no one else; for there is no other name under heaven that has been given among men by which we must be saved."* (Acts 4:12)

> *"Therefore let all the house of Israel know for certain that God has made Him both Lord and Christ—this Jesus whom you crucified.*
> *Now when they heard this, they were pierced to the heart, and said to Peter and the rest of the apostles, 'Brethren, what shall we do?' Peter said to them, 'Repent, and each of you be baptized in the name of Jesus Christ for*

the forgiveness of your sins; and you will receive the gift of the Holy Spirit. For the promise is for you and your children and for all who are far off, as many as the Lord our God will call to Himself.' And with many other words he solemnly testified and kept on exhorting them, saying, 'Be saved from this perverse generation!' So then, those who had received his word were baptized; and that day there were added about three thousand souls. They were continually devoting themselves to the apostles' teaching and to fellowship, to the breaking of bread and to prayer.

Everyone kept feeling a sense of awe; and many wonders and signs were taking place through the apostles. And all those who had believed were together and had all things in common; and they began selling their property and possessions and were sharing them with all, as anyone might have need. Day by day continuing with one mind in the temple, and breaking bread from house to house, they were taking their meals together with gladness and sincerity of heart, praising God and having favor with all the people. And the Lord was adding to their number day by day those who were being saved." (Acts 2:36-47)

"I am writing to you, little children, because your sins have been forgiven you for His name's sake." (1 John 2:12)

"Go therefore and make disciples of all the nations, baptizing them in the name of the Father and the Son and the Holy Spirit" (Matthew 28:19)

From the Scriptures above, we can see that we receive remission of sins through baptism in His name, the name of our everlasting Father, Jesus Christ. The Word of God itself refers to our Lord Jesus Christ as our Father.

"For a child will be born to us, a son will be given to us; and the government will rest on His shoulders; and His

name will be called Wonderful Counselor, Mighty God, Eternal Father, Prince of Peace." (Isaiah 9:6)

I decided to get baptized in Jesus' name because I no longer wanted to live in sin, and I wanted to be cleansed and freed from sin. A 13-year-old girl, who still hadn't experienced a lot in life, no longer wanted to live in sin. That was true then and it's true to this day, even though I went through my season of being a prodigal daughter myself. I've been set free from the sin that had a hold on my life at that young age. If the Lord Jesus Christ, can do it for me, He can do it for you, as well.

OUR HUMBLE FATHER

It takes humility to accept and obey the Lord Jesus Christ as our Heavenly Father; to receive the wisdom and knowledge He gives to direct and guide us in our lives. It takes humility to understand that He does it all for our own good; not to be controlling or a master over us, but rather as a Father. Although, He is a Master and we are His servants, He still humbles Himself not to take the role of dictator. Instead, He tries to form a relationship with us so that He can be the loving, teaching, and correcting Father, who gave everything He had for us.

As our Heavenly Father, doesn't He deserve our full love, respect and obedience? As His children, will He not love us, correct us, teach us and give us everything we need so that one day we will live with Him forever? Imagine never having to lose your father. We will never have to mourn the loss of our Heavenly Father, Jesus Christ. He is alive and eternal; He never leaves nor forsakes His children.

For some, He's the Father you never had and He wants to adopt you as His own. He wants to take you under His wing and fill that void in your life. Maybe some feel they don't need their father or they're better off without him. In some cases, that may be true, but it will never be true for our Heavenly Father. He is the reason we are alive and breathing right now. An earthly father helps create life, but he cannot sustain life. Our Heavenly Father not only gives us the breath of life, but He continues to supply it until our time on this earth is complete. Without Him, we would not wake up every morning; He is the Creator and supplier of all life.

> *"The God who made the world and all things in it, since He is Lord of heaven and earth, does not dwell in temples made with hands; nor is He served by human hands, as though He needed anything, since He Himself gives to all people life and breath and all things; and He made from one man every nation of mankind to live on all the face of the earth, having determined their appointed times and the boundaries of their habitation, that they would seek God, if perhaps they might grope for Him and find Him, though He is not far from each one of us; for in Him we live and move and exist, as even some of your own poets have said, 'For we also are His children.'"* (Acts 17:24-28)

> *"Who among all these does not know that the hand of the LORD has done this, in whose hand is the life of every living thing, and the breath of all mankind?"* (Job 12:9-10)

> *"Yet you, his son, Belshazzar, have not humbled your heart, even though you knew all this, but you have exalted yourself against the Lord of heaven; and they have brought the*

vessels of His house before you, and you and your nobles, your wives and your concubines have been drinking wine from them; and you have praised the gods of silver and gold, of bronze, iron, wood and stone, which do not see, hear or understand. But the God in whose hand are your life-breath and all your ways, you have not glorified."
(Daniel 5:22-23)

Once again, it takes humility to understand and accept that even as adults we are still living under our Father's roof. In the following verses, King Solomon tells us the instructions he received from his father, King David. Understanding and believing that the Bible is written by men who were inspired by the Spirit of God, we can know that this is written to demonstrate what a father desires and is trying to teach his child and what our Heavenly Father desires to teach us.

"Hear, O sons, the instruction of a father, and give attention that you may gain understanding, for I give you sound teaching; do not abandon my instruction. When I was a son to my father, tender and the only son in the sight of my mother, then he taught me and said to me, 'Let your heart hold fast my words; keep my commandments and live; acquire wisdom! Acquire understanding! Do not forget nor turn away from the words of my mouth. Do not forsake her, and she will guard you; love her, and she will watch over you. The beginning of wisdom is: acquire wisdom; and with all your acquiring, get understanding. Prize her, and she will exalt you; she will honor you if you embrace her. She will place on your head a garland of grace; she will present you with a crown of beauty.'

Hear, my son, and accept my sayings and the years of your life will be many. I have directed you in the way of wisdom; I have led you in upright paths. When you walk, your steps will not be impeded; and if you run, you will not stumble. Take hold of instruction; do not let go. Guard her, for she is your life. Do not enter the path of the wicked and do not proceed in the way of evil men. Avoid it, do not pass by it; turn away from it and pass on. For they cannot sleep unless they do evil; and they are robbed of sleep unless they make someone stumble. For they eat the bread of wickedness and drink the wine of violence. But the path of the righteous is like the light of dawn, that shines brighter and brighter until the full day. The way of the wicked is like darkness; they do not know over what they stumble.

My son, give attention to my words; incline your ear to my sayings. Do not let them depart from your sight; keep them in the midst of your heart. For they are life to those who find them and health to all their body. Watch over your heart with all diligence, for from it flow the springs of life. Put away from you a deceitful mouth and put devious speech far from you. Let your eyes look directly ahead and let your gaze be fixed straight in front of you. Watch the path of your feet and all your ways will be established. Do not turn to the right nor to the left; turn your foot from evil." (Proverbs 4:1-27)

The God of the universe doesn't have to take our shortcomings or failures; He doesn't have to put up with our pride and rebellion. Thankfully, He is loving and patient; He is a disciplinary, yet merciful. All of these qualities make Him the perfect Father, who is raising children for His kingdom. Let's seek to know and love the Lord Jesus Christ, so that we can see Him as the Father that He is.

"The Lord is not slow about His promise, as some count slowness, but is patient toward you, not willing for any to perish, but for all to come to repentance." (2 Peter 3:9)

ACKNOWLEDGEMENTS

I would like to thank my Lord Jesus Christ for guiding me through this book, from start to finish. I'm so thankful and blessed to be a chosen vessel, in spite of my weaknesses. All glory and honor goes to Him alone.

I also want to thank my family, church family and loved ones for their constant love, support, and spiritual encouragement. Whether you helped me edit, gave me your input, or simply prayed for me, I greatly appreciate you and thank you. If any of you did not even know I was writing this book—surprise! Please know that all of you were in my heart during this process. I love each and every one of you.

REFERENCES

Fast, Stephanie. Broadcast. *Healing Childhood Traumas*. Colorado Springs, CO: Focus on the Family, December 9, 1986.